THE ACCIDENTAL
GARDENER

Michael Powell

summersdale

THE ACCIDENTAL GARDENER
1st edition printed in 2003
This 2nd edition © Summersdale Publishers Ltd, 2004
Text by Michael Powell

Summersdale Publishers Ltd
46 West Street
Chichester
West Sussex
PO19 1RP
UK

www.summersdale.com

Printed and bound in Great Britain.

ISBN: 1 84024 423 2

THE ACCIDENTAL GARDENER

JANUARY

January brings rain and rime
Snowdrops under frost do sleep
A Christmas tree that's past its prime
Lies naked on the compost heap

Another year begins in this extraordinary cycle of birth, death and rebirth. On a crisp January morning, take a moment to ponder new beginnings while you stuff a desiccated poinsettia and a seven-foot Douglas fir into your wheely bin.

It was Hans Christian Andersen who said that merely living is not enough and that one must have sunshine, freedom and a little flower in order to thrive. But remember that there are no flowers without tools, and no tools without a garage to keep them in. Which brings us to the first job of the year.

Rescue your tools from under the pile of junk that has accumulated in your garage during the winter. Clean them with a John Innes oily rag number 2. While searching you will discover a forgotten box of mouldy dahlias, glads and other bulbs that you dutifully wintered in your damp garage. Throw them away. Arrange for the cutting blades on your lawnmower to be sharpened. Shop for a new model when you discover it's been stolen, along with most of your tools. Fix the lock on your garage.

The days are short and the nights can be very chilly. For wildlife, the need to find food means that even the most timid birds and mammals are active and those that are normally nocturnal may venture out in daylight if the weather gets really bleak. This makes it an ideal time to down the bottle of Stag's Breath that was left over from New Year's Eve and spend the misty afternoons sitting in your greenhouse taking pot shots at badgers and hedgehogs.

January is the time for making ambitious plans and dreaming about winning gold medals at the Chelsea Flower Show. Ask your eight-year-old son to demonstrate the Garden Planner CD-ROM he bought you for Christmas. Plant heather, jasmine and other winter-flowering shrubs now. Seed pansies, geraniums and other early flowers. Get a refund on the CD-ROM when it 'fails to install on Windows 3.1'. Curl up with a goodly pile of traditional and reliable plant and seed catalogues. Buy new tools, lawnmower and multimedia PC.

If you are a beginner who feels overwhelmed by the choice of gardening equipment, here are the basics you will need to get started:

One short pointy thing for poking out weeds.

One long pointy thing for poking out weeds when your back is sore.

One small container for putting weeds in.

One large container (e.g. a wheely bin) for emptying the small container when it is full of weeds.

A can of petrol to start a bonfire when your wheely bin is full.

Every gardener has a favourite piece of kit, whether it is a hoe, gloves or weeding cushion. But choosing the right gardening apparel is even more important. Have you noticed how builders always wear designer shirts? Make sure you wear the most expensive clothing you can afford to get muddy in. You want to make a statement that says: 'expensive-durable'. If your neighbour sees you getting down and dirty in a £125 Burberry polo shirt, he'll presume that you own twenty more.

In January the garden looks somewhat bare but there are a few places that you may enjoy visiting where nature's magnificence is always present. Stay indoors and surf the Internet on your new PC.

Why not use these winter months to bone up on your Latin? The system of naming plants and flowers in Latin is not as complex as it may first seem. The words are descriptive of colour, habitat, season, scent, growth and aesthetic. You need only learn twenty Latin words to have an impressive vocabulary at your *digitalis endia*.

For example, a green flower from the southern hemisphere might be described as *viridis australis*. A green plant that spreads would be called *viridis patens* (which, let's face it, you can use to describe most plants); 'red and fragrant' is *rubens fragrens*; while *feris pastoralis* means 'wild and grows in pastures'. S*ementem* requires little maintenance; *acid lounge* thrives indoors with a soil pH lower than 7; and a phrase that will appear frequently in this book, *naboreus gardenia,* hardly needs any translation.

If you don't want to bother learning all those Latin names, memorise some of the track listings from a Jimi Hendrix album. There are several plausible examples on *Voodoo Child*: Purple Haze, Little Wing, Spanish Castle Magic, Foxy Lady, Wild Thing, Izabella, Dolly Dagger.

THOUGHTS FOR JANUARY

Whoever said that watering in the midday sun can burn plants must have been suffering from rabies. Water cannot burn anything. In fact, it is widely recognised as an effective way of putting out fires.

Always remember your garden is unique, just like everyone else's.

FEBRUARY

The crocus is the first to bloom
While winter's icy frosts hold sway
Fooling you that spring comes soon
Even though it's ages away

There's an old Russian proverb that says that more grows in the garden than the gardener sows – referring, of course, to every gardener's worst enemy: weeds. When the year's first weeds and pests start to appear, it's important to get in a pre-emptive strike to prevent them from overwhelming you later. If you try to hoe out weeds, you'll end up knee-deep in claggy mud. The neatest solution is to rent a hydraulic PTO with a heavy-duty, stainless steel 500-gallon spray tank, a 35 GPM positive displacement pump, 0–800 PSI pressure gauge and powerful mechanical agitation. Open the lounge window, put some Wagner on the hi-fi and go into battle!

There are as many methods of trying to make your garden pest-free as there are ways to smuggle spent plutonium out of the former Soviet Union. Your local petro-chemical by-product outlet will happily sell you a barrel of toxic mulch to spread on your roses. Spread thickly to ensure coverage. Do not choose selective weedkillers because studies show they don't kill everything. Remember the gardener's lore that it is better to obliterate any suggestion of wildlife than to salvage the plant it might cling to. If you start finding dead squirrels, moles and deer in your garden, or hear local news reports that the water table has been contaminated, then you'll know you've done a thorough job.

Gardeners always try to outdo each other with their ability to name hitherto unheard of menaces, the implication being that they've already taken swift action to eradicate pests that you didn't even know existed, while your garden is undoubtedly infested. What novice gardeners don't realise is that most of these names are made up by adding the word 'fly', 'mite', 'spot' or 'weevil' to the end of any word, usually a colour. Hence sawfly, whitefly, greenfly, blackspot, lawnmite, shedfly, fencemite, arseweevil, etc.

Most seed packets contain more than a hundred seeds. But do you really intend to plant 125 sunflowers this spring? Instead, save thirty or so and next time someone asks you for money in the street, reply: 'I will not give you money, for surely you will spend it on junk food and alcohol, but please accept this seed with my love.'

Your winter-flowering pansies need a bright, sunny position to develop maximum blooms. Though heaven knows how this is supposed to happen while the weather is still so unpredictable. Start dusting your houseplants again once they begin to show signs of new growth and keep reminding yourself that your Seasonal Affective Disorder will soon improve.

You have spent January browsing through seed catalogues, but now is the time to order annual and perennial seeds for spring planting. (An annual is a plant that dies after one season, a perennial comes back year after year if it doesn't die first.)

Start stealing your favourite cuttings from your *naboreus gardenia*.

Make sure you protect the young shoots emerging from your lawn in areas where you have planted daffodils. Children and dogs should now be locked in the house until November.

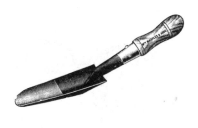

Prepare vegetable plots. Use well-decomposed garden compost and plant your potato crops. Then ask yourself why you just spent seven hours digging to nurture such a cheap and boring vegetable. Next year, plant asparagus beds instead or erect a fibreglass pagoda.

Inspect your trees and shrubs and nail on any branches damaged by winter storms. Cut off any branches from your neighbour's trees that are overhanging your property and either throw them over the fence or dump them in his skip.

There are many ways to create the illusion of space in a small garden. The best of these is pruning. Prune fruit trees and other evergreens now. Most plants benefit from hard pruning. The naked beauty of *Salix x rubens 'Basfordiana'* makes them a radiant presence in any winter border. Enjoy them now, but prune the suckers back to their stubby little bases to teach them some humility. As a general rule of thumb, you should prune as close to the ground as your tools will allow. If you've received a chainsaw for Christmas, then hard prune now in preparation for laying decking and a large plastic garden chess set.

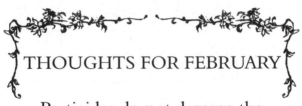

THOUGHTS FOR FEBRUARY

Pesticides do not damage the environment. They are merely chemicals in the wrong place.

When in doubt, dig and burn.

MARCH

Spring is near and yet more rain
As flash frosts kill the early shoots
This miserable climate is insane
We trudge around in wellington boots

Lift and divide large clumps of herbaceous plants. Replant the three remaining tiny specimens after removing enough old woody stalks to fill your neighbour's skip. Buy an amusing Gandalf gargoyle or a small Japanese ornamental bridge to plug the gap.

Prepare for regular mowing. Your lawn will begin to grow rapidly now and will fill you with pride for several days in mid-April, before ants, pets and children render it indistinguishable from a Northern Counties League soccer pitch.

Did you know that ducks are natural predators of slugs? As the old saying goes, if you have too many slugs the chances are you have a deficiency of ducks. So buy a pair this month and you'll soon be hooked on duck keeping.

Always wear sturdy shoes or boots when gardening. You never know when your neighbour is going to come round and demand that you stop throwing your garden rubbish into his skip. And when punches start flying, it's always a blessing to find you're wearing your favourite pair of 10-eyelet leather boots with three-row stitches and steel toecaps. They also provide much-needed protection when he unleashes his Staffordshire bull terrier.

This month your mother will come to stay for a week. She will insist on having the heating on full power, and the combination of dry heat and over-watering from a bored and interfering relative will kill most of your houseplants. Expect to miss the first of the new series of *Real Gardens* on Channel 4 while she slavers over Trevor Eve pouting his way through yet another cop drama on BBC1.

Choose a bright, crisp March morning to drop in to your solicitor on your way back from the garden centre. Now spring is finally here, it's time to rekindle the boundary dispute that appears to have cooled off during the winter. Also, stay alert for holes in the hedge to stop the ducks from escaping into your *naboreus gardenia*.

Your fancy mail-order pelargoniums should have arrived by now. Pot them up and put them in the conservatory. If you don't have a conservatory, then try spending a little less time in the garden and concentrate on impressing your boss. If you're already retired, then it's way too late.

Net out the duckweed from the pond (this must be done frequently, or it will completely cover the surface of the water and block out sunlight). On second thoughts, why bother when your shubunkin and ghost koi were snatched by a heron last October leaving you three oversized golden orfe… and where's the sun anyway?

Frogs, newts and children will also appear in the pond this month. It doesn't matter how many times you tell a child to stay away from water, they can't resist trying to drown themselves. If it wasn't for the ducks, you could fill in the pond with large pebbles until the children are older. You may choose an ingenious compromise and fill your children's pockets with so many pebbles that they can't get off the sofa.

Incidentally, it isn't necessary to spend money on a fountain to oxygenate the water in your pond. Just throw the cat in every morning. Allow him to thrash around helplessly for five minutes before pulling him out again. He will benefit from the vigorous exercise and will aerate the pond at the same time.

Expect the weather to be a mixed bag this month. A very mild spell mid-month will encourage burgeoning growth everywhere, but will be followed by two nights of sub-zero temperatures that will kill everything off again.

Don't be surprised if around this time you suffer third-degree burns after attempting to start a bonfire using the gallon of petrol you siphoned from your neighbour's 4 x 4. As you convalesce in your garden, you may also suffer minor facial injuries after walking into one of the support canes for your sweet peas.

THOUGHTS FOR MARCH

Railway sleepers are not decorative
border features. They are squalid
and ugly reminders of the
industrial revolution.

Don't use force. Use a bigger tool.

APRIL

Spring-like sunshine warms the ground
To wintertime we bid adieu
Pests and weeds do now confound
April showers cause damage too

Did you know that there are some 60 varieties of bee native to the UK? Why not take up the fascinating and productive hobby of bee-keeping? Bees are only dangerous if you don't know what you're doing.

Aerate, scarify and feed the lawn with high-nitrogen fertiliser and re-seed where the grass is thin. Use a spreader to ensure the fertiliser is spread evenly, but don't get your hopes up because within weeks the combination of children and duck droppings will make it look like you've just hosted the Bath and West Show.

Even though the ducks have virtually rid your garden of slugs, a freak hailstorm in the middle of the month will devastate your succulents. Your crassulas and hostas will look like they've been napalmed. To add to the carnage, a pack of confused foxhounds, thrown off-scent by your prize collection of *Fritillaria imperialis*, will stampede through your garden sending the ducks into a catatonic trance.

Now that the ducks have been taken into care, return to your customary method of spreading broken glass around your perennials, bulbs, ground cover, trees and shrubs (and especially your hostas) to protect from slugs and snails.

The weather is warm enough for you to take some of your conservatory plants outside now, especially the date palm and *Eupatorium sordidum*. However, don't be surprised if two days later someone steals them, along with a fibreglass sundial and your new lawnmower. Remember to keep your garage locked at all times. You wouldn't have minded if someone had stolen the rhododendron 'April Glow' which now bursts into life with a flock of garish pink flowers. Chain up the rest of your outdoor pots.

About this time, expect the annual gift of an Easter lily from your mother. Place it in indirect sunlight, away from drafts and don't overwater it. Reflect bitterly how every year she kills off your houseplants and then tries to poison your cat. Repeatedly drop hints that Easter lilies are highly toxic, and remain vigilant for signs of feline kidney failure.

Keep a close eye on fruit trees at this time of year. If you suspect that they are infected with aphids, use a 15,000 PSI hydrodynamic industrial water jet to dislodge them. This is best done early to allow leaves and branches time to regrow.

THOUGHTS FOR APRIL

Topiary is not a rewarding hobby that allows for creativity and individuality in the garden. It is the recourse of obsessive-compulsives and shows less imagination than a person who collects their toenail clippings and owns a large ball made out of rubber bands.

Removing the top four rungs of your ladder will make it safer.

MAY

Lilac and cherry are in bloom
And all the leaves are on the trees
Snails continue to consume
Your hostas in large quantities

Ah, doesn't it feel marvellous when everything is flowering and warm weather beckons? Take some time to walk round the garden taking it all in and enjoying seeing everything looking so fruitful.

Fill in any unsightly empty spaces between border perennials. It's not too late to seed some hardy annuals straight into their flowering positions. For a quick solution that provides interest and colour, tie party balloons in clumps. Also, pepper the border with little signs on which you have printed pithy or humorous gardening quotes.

You may get a pleasant surprise when a few glads and dahlias spring up from corms that you planted last year and forgot to lift. Gardening is full of little miracles like this. Plants can survive over winter without protection, whereas your garage seems to have the kiss of death when it comes to storing anything.

Now all danger of frost has gone, transplant your Easter lily outside in a sunny part of the garden and celebrate that your cat has survived this latest assassination attempt.

The best time to pick flowers from your garden is in the early morning. The best time to pick them from your *naboreus gardenia* is when he's on holiday – still a little early yet, then. Although it is the perfect time to paint little orange spots on the leaves of his fruit trees.

An hour in the garden puts life's problems into perspective. Relax! Lie down and enjoy the sounds and smells of your neighbour burning a large pile of branches that he has hastily removed from his fruit trees. Before you drop off to sleep, allow yourself to muse upon this month's Chelsea Flower Show and hazily remember last year's trend of creating 'natural' gardens with borders peppered with flowers on the turn. You wake up after a refreshing sleep and switch on Radio 4 to hear news that Prince Charles' compost heap has just won a gold medal.

It is by no means essential to grow all vegetables from seed. You can also buy them from the supermarket where you can find fully-grown vegetables of all kinds – even out of season.

Plants are living things, and like other living things – you, your cat, children, parents – they have their foibles and preferences. If you treat your plants like members of your family, they will thrive. But you mustn't get sentimental when it's time to stuff them in the wheely bin. Evergreen shrubs that have been severely damaged by frost drop their leaves and often look dead. Some experts advise you not to discard any plants unless you are sure there are no vital signs. When Nietzsche talked about the 'will to flower' he was talking about his half-hardy artemisias. And the Old Testament is forever going on about separating the wheat from the chaff. It is precisely these life and death decisions that define you as a gardener. So show no mercy. If weak plants can't hack it, then they don't deserve a place in your garden.

THOUGHTS FOR MAY

Pesticides boost the economy as we spend an estimated £30 million every year on them, and provide jobs for the people who sell them.

Don't carry hatred in your heart. Use a wheelbarrow.

JUNE

With longer days and shorter nights
Sweet garden scents now fill the air
The skin on your forehead feels less tight
And you've regrown most of your hair

'What is so rare as a day in June?' wrote the poet James Russell Lowell. He must have spent his summers in a cardboard box, since this is the month with the greatest hours of daylight in the year. But the sentiment is understood. Summer has arrived at last!

Don't be impatient. Often it takes time to see the results of your hard work in the garden. The exception to this rule is pruning, where you can achieve instant gratification. If you've got a dirty little leaf-dropping evergreen magnolia then hard prune to the ground. But after this month that's your lot until the autumn, although hedges may need trimming. Still, you've been dropping hints that you'd like a rotary cultivator for your birthday next month, so at least you can get to work on re-turfing your lawn soon.

A garden is a very visceral place – a place of discovery, an opening to spiritual experiences and one of the few places left in our modern world where we can be ourselves. However, there's nothing spiritual about pruning. Keep your clothes on and always use a residual circuit breaker.

Remember to turn the golden orfe twice a week, as the same view can get very boring for large fish in a small pond.

Don't go out on the razzle every Saturday night. A dedicated gardener often spends time out in the garden instead, hand pollinating his plants.

If you suffer from insomnia or sleepwalking (or just like hanging around in your garden after dark under the pretext of doing a spot of watering in the hope that one day you'll catch a glimpse of your neighbour's wife taking a shower), there are lots of plants you can buy that actually flower at dusk or at night. These include evening primrose, sweet-scented nicotiana, moonflowers, night phlox and angel's trumpet.

If you have a bird feeder in your garden, remove it now. You just kept the birds on the breadline over the winter. Now it's pay-back time and you don't want to encourage a fast-food mentality among your bird life. Neither do you want flabby feeders – only lean and mean birds will eat the butterflies that are a continual annoyance at this time of year. Likewise, make sure your bird feeder is within easy reach of your cat – another way of ensuring that natural selection favours alert and hardy bird specimens.

THOUGHTS FOR JUNE

The Yorkshire proverb 'A dog, a wife, and a walnut tree: the more you beat them, the better they be', is misleading. Walnut trees show little improvement after a good thrashing.

Clean boots are often a sign of muddy knees.

JULY

The sun beats down all through the day
Till everything turns brown and dry
Unless you use the hose to spray
You'd better kiss your plants goodbye

Whoever said that to be happy for an hour you should get drunk but to be happy for a lifetime, plant a garden, missed an obvious opportunity: to get drunk *and* plant a garden. Or in your case, a lawn. Take a week off work and follow this advice (actually from Goethe) to begin putting your dreams into action. Especially as it's your birthday this month and you'll be receiving a slew of gardening-related gifts. Celebrate by heading off to the pub, proudly wearing your new 'I'd rather be gardening' T-shirt.

Return six hours later and begin to blithely strip away your beleaguered turf with your new rotary cultivator. Then, as your neighbour parks his car on 'your' drive and starts waving his fists, you'll soon realise you've dug up the wrong lawn. Often nature teaches us hard lessons. A happy gardener is a sober one.

After a day in bed with the worst hangover of your life, why not spend the rest of the week re-turfing the lawn in your *naboreus gardenia*. You can't afford to shell out for another load of turf for yourself so it looks like you're stuck with the old feed and weed for another year.

Bark chippings make an ideal all-purpose mulch. And there's no need to buy bags of it from the garden centre. Take a look around your garden – it's likely that you have a home-grown supply on your trees. Chiselling bark from the trees in your own garden is something the whole family can enjoy. It saves a few pennies, plus it's environmentally friendly.

You may have the worst lawn in the world, but this shouldn't stop you from having the best barbecue ever! Building a barbecue is a relatively easy project, requiring a minimum amount of skill and DIY knowledge. Give your odd-jobber mate Brian a ring and ask him to fix you up with the raw materials.

Begin by digging a small trench, approximately 12 inches wide by 9 inches deep, in the shape that you want your barbecue. When your spade unearths two human phalanges, phone the police immediately. It's probably nothing, but it's best to play safe. Don't panic if they cordon off the area and ask you to accompany them to the station. You have a clear conscience and they will release you without charge within eight hours. Return home and take a break from gardening for several days – at least until the police have finished excavating and have removed the large white tent that covered your entire garden. Also, close the curtains to prevent unwanted attention from the world's media, which is camping outside.

The police enquiry will soon extend into your *naboreus gardenia* and you'll be shocked and also secretly overjoyed when he is arrested for murder. Police searching his garden shed will also uncover a large hoard of stolen property, including two lawnmowers, tools, several dead pot plants and a sundial. By now your garden will have been destroyed, but an exclusive deal with one of the tabloids and compensation from the police will ensure that you can take a week's holiday in Sorrento to recover from your ordeal. You'll have enough money left to plant the garden from scratch when you return, so your Garden Planner CD-ROM can really come into its own.

Expect to return home with a nice tan and a vision. You are going to plant the garden of your dreams: a full-blown Italian Renaissance garden with flights of steps, statues and fountains, complete with a row of cypress trees, vines and a bijou lemon grove. The layout of the entrance and exit will be in a north-south direction and the outer boundary of the garden will be delineated by a circular sheared yew hedge. At the centre of the garden a formal pond with fountains will be edged by pebble inlaid pavers, and finally, nestling within the outer circular hedge of the garden will be a Gandalf gargoyle, a plastic sundial and a small Japanese ornamental bridge (it's a shame to let them go to waste).

However, if you pop round to introduce yourself to your new neighbour, you'll be bound to blurt out your ambitious plans and discover that he works for the council. He'll point out that you'll be unlikely to get planning permission. So, it'll be back to the drawing board while cursing yet another smart-arse neighbour.

THOUGHTS FOR JULY

That which we call a rose by any other name would smell as sweet. But would buying a dozen Old Men's Fistulas for your valentine still be a romantic gesture?

If at first you don't succeed, have a bonfire with what's left.

AUGUST

A summer breeze blows up the dust
Late summer days are spent outdoors
Every garden in August
Has plants and flowers, except for yours

So, here you are at the end of summer with a *tabula rasa* which is gardener's Latin for 'environmental disaster'. All you have to show for seven months' hard labour is a large sheet of black plastic pinned down with the bricks that you were going to use to build the barbecue. It seems that wherever you go people are gushing about how *marvellous* their garden is at this time of year.

You resolve to host a bring a plant and a bottle party, the idea being that everyone can come along, eat a burger, have a few drinks and then help you replant your garden. You might even get to do a bit of seeding of your own, if you get lucky. Unfortunately, only five people turn up and one of those is your mother. And, surprise surprise, she's brought with her a selection of highly feline-toxic plants: caladium, dieffenbachia, philodendron, ivy and azalea.

Every August your mother invites you to the Southport Flower Show for two days. This year, while you are away, the *Ground Force* team are busy creating the minimalist garden of your nightmares. You return home with a boot load of your favourite plants to be greeted by a grinning Alan Titchmarsh as he springs out from behind one of six enormous stainless steel planters. The rest of your property is covered with limestone, decking and black bamboo. When you start crying, everyone thinks you are weeping tears of joy and they start hugging each other and drinking champagne.

A familiar summer weather pattern now emerges: blistering sun during the week while you are at work and then torrential rain every weekend. The only bit of sun you see is when you have to rush home from work one afternoon because your son has crashed his bike into one of the steel planters and broken his arm. Enough is enough. After you return from casualty, you phone the BBC and demand that they return the garden to its former condition. And so you can end the month the same way that you began.

Except that now it's raining again. But every cloud has a silver lining. Spend a wet Saturday afternoon in your local records office and you may be rewarded with the discovery of a seventeenth-century deed showing evidence of an ancient bridleway through your new neighbour's garden. Ask your solicitor to send him a letter notifying him of your intention to make full use of it in the future.

Also, you won't have to tolerate the high-pitched screams of swifts for much longer. These annoying little creatures will not be able to fly low overhead on long summer evenings for much longer. The cold weather will force them to fly off to Africa.

THOUGHTS FOR AUGUST

Gardeners wear wide-brimmed hats
not to protect them from the
elements, but to let others know
that their grubby fingernails are the
result of recreational rather than
blue-collar pursuits.

Never let a bonfire know
you're in a hurry.

SEPTEMBER

September brings the ripening fruit
And windfalls from the boughs are blown
Now every garden doth transmute
Except for your disaster zone

Come on! It's time to strip away the black plastic and get planting before the clocks go back and Seasonal Affective Disorder creeps into your life again. When the going gets tough, the tough gets growin'! If you feel barely borderline functional now, just think how depressed you are going to be staring at a giant bin-liner in the depths of winter. This has been an unpredictable year, but who said that gardening was easy? Perhaps it's time to throw in the trowel and pay someone else to do the job.

Choosing the right garden contractor can add considerable value to your home. Find someone with excellent references who is enthusiastic about the work. Make sure you agree a price with your mate Brian before he starts. Don't accept vague reassurances like 'Just buy me a few drinks'.

When Brian fails to show up for a week, go round the pub and try to find out where he is. Return home and give him one more day to sort out his attitude.

Sack 'Incapability Brian' (as you have now christened him) when he turns up three days later and tries to sell you a lawnmower. Your only option now is to do the whole thing yourself.

The first stage of planning involves assessing existing features. In your case: a large brick barbecue, a boot load of plants from Southport, some cat poison and one very large fish (looks like there just wasn't enough room for three – did you remember to keep turning them regularly?).

Take a handful of dirt and rub it between your finger and thumb. This is called 'understanding your soil'. Soil, like water, is the source of all life on the planet. If it slips through your fingers and blows away in the wind, it is sandy; if you could use it to make ashtrays and other small decorative items, it is clay. Anything in between is called 'filthy loam'.

Now that you understand your soil, the next trick is to find out what you can grow well, and grow lots of it. Make a list of ten things you grow well, then plant the top three everywhere. You may think that a garden full of leylandii, mint and crocosmia might get a little boring, but at least you know they'll survive. Then pick one unusual specimen plant for a conversation piece, and don't shy away from heirloom plants or accessories. For example, a macramé planter or little wooden wheelbarrow can be a classic and timeless feature. Remember to keep everything well watered (this is called 'damping on').

If your plants seem happy, keep doing what you're doing. If they're not thriving then dig them up and threaten them with the compost heap. Then replant and watch carefully for a couple of weeks. If they still don't shape up, throw them away and try something else. Life's too short to grow prima donnas.

With a chill in the air you'll notice the birds are more active. Large gangs will rampage noisily through the garden each morning. Robins become particularly aggressive at this time of year, as they will soon be pairing up and defending their territory. It's best to turn up the radio if you are easily offended by the sounds of copulating *Erithacus rubecula*. The Americans don't call this little pest *Turdus migratorius* for nothing.

Noisy birds aside, this can be a wonderful time for sitting in your garden and appreciating the unique mellow, golden light of September. Your trees are already firing up their autumn tints and giving your garden a pleasing, apocalyptic quality that makes you yearn for winter when everything has died back and you can stop mowing the lawn for four months.

THOUGHTS FOR SEPTEMBER

People who garden regularly do not live longer, it's just that many pensioners draw attention to themselves by the very act of being in their gardens. There are many older folk whom you never see because the secret of their longevity is to sit inside in their pyjamas all day watching TV.

Instead of waiting for someone to bring you flowers, pick them from someone else's garden.

OCTOBER

Autumn colours please the senses
October weather starts to grate
Gusting winds blow down your fences
It makes you want to emigrate

Collect the first falling leaves of the season and dump them on the surface of the pond. This will mulch the fish over winter while providing camouflage protection against herons and other opportunistic predators. Then build your own leaf shredder for subsequent leaf falls, so that you can give your composting a head start. Cut a hole in the top of one of your lawnmowers and mount it on an old water tank that's sitting in the garage. It will also have an added benefit of being a cheap and effective dog scarer.

When one of your fence posts and panels inevitably gets blown down this month, it will make you marvel at what an amazing piece of machinery the human body is. An eighty-year-old woman wearing slippers can stand perfectly easily in a force six gale without being blown over, and without having to bury herself up to her knees in cement and hard-core. However, you must dig a hole at least two feet deep to hold a replacement eight-foot post.

Did you know that one tree can remove 26 pounds of carbon dioxide from the atmosphere annually, equalling 11,000 miles of car emissions? So, if you have at least one tree in your garden and are an average car user, you needn't worry about polluting the atmosphere.

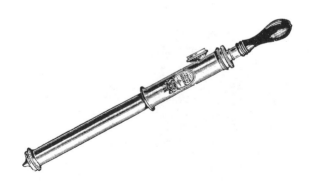

Before planting your daffodils, give the bulbs a good squeeze. If the bulb is soft, this may indicate that it is harbouring the larva of a bulb fly. Microwave on full power for 60 seconds and then plant.

Did you know that bonsai means 'a plant growing in a container'? So if anyone asks you if you've ever kept bonsai you can probably answer 'Yes' truthfully.

At Hallowe'en, impress your children's friends by explaining that there is no such thing as a pumpkin because they are in fact certain varieties of squash of the family *Cucurbitaceae*, which for complex etymological reasons that you won't bore them with, have come to be called pumpkins. Also, amaze them by revealing that an onion is a type of lily, and show them your collection of witty gardening slogan T-shirts.

THOUGHTS FOR OCTOBER

Give a man a fish and he will eat for a
day. Give him a packet of seeds and he
will throw them back at you and say,
'What the hell do you expect me
to do with those?'

Behind every cloud is blue sky,
but you can't see it because
of the cloud.

NOVEMBER

Now take stock as winter comes
And perennials are all but gone
How brave that the chrysanthemums
Refuse to die and struggle on

Ah, the winter garden. Two words that conjure up images of drab seaside resorts struggling to attract off-season custom. But this year, bring some mystical charm into your life. Wind chimes can be decorative and symbolic features. These simple and elegant musical sculptures help disperse negative energy, scare away evil spirits and tell you when the wind is blowing.

With the usual torrents of rain this month, expect to be told that it's once again been the wettest autumn since records began in 1760-something. (Before then everyone was too busy throwing sewage into the street and dying from consumption to notice anything as frivolous as the weather. This mid-eighteenth-century meteorological milestone was a very important sociological indicator. Or maybe it was the date that jam jars were invented.)

Stay indoors and watch predictable news footage of publicans piling up sandbags, pensioners in pyjamas poking their heads out of first-floor windows, and canoeists smugly paddling around as if this was the way things were meant to be. God would never send another flood to wipe out humankind, because he knows a bunch of canoeists would always survive to repopulate the planet. The effect of all this rain, of course, is to turn the garden into a paddy field and bonfire night will once again bring the NHS to its knees as parents nationwide attempt to relight damp fireworks.

In between the heavy showers, speed up decomposition in your compost heap by turning it every fortnight. If you manage to shoot any herons, just fork them into the mix. It really doesn't matter what you put on it. Many gardeners are quite picky about this, and won't compost weeds or diseased plants in the misguided belief that a compost heap can remain a seed- and pest-free oasis. A compost heap is merely a *momento mori* or a thought-provoking sacred place to remind the gardener that in the midst of life he or she is in death – a place of decay that provides a symbolic counterpoint to the life-force present elsewhere in the garden. Rather like an old man coughing at the back of the church during a christening service.

Another thing you can do indoors this month is to create your own genetically modified plants. Take a few seeds and zap them in your microwave oven to jostle the genes around. It's a hit or miss process, but you'll be amazed at some of the Frankenstein flowers this method can produce. You may even hit the jackpot and grow some killer tomatoes.

THOUGHTS FOR NOVEMBER

Hard work pays off in the future.
Laziness pays off now.

Do not celebrate that thorns have
roses. Roses have thorns. Do hernias
have people?

DECEMBER

Gardening is just like life
It grips us hard until the grave
Full of disappointment, dirt and strife
And we are its unwilling slave

Rediscover your greenhouse, which you probably haven't used since January, and as another gardening year draws to a close, take a moment to reflect upon what you have achieved. Remember the Zen saying: Sitting quiet, doing nothing, spring comes, and the grass grows by itself. Hmmm. Has it really been worth all the effort?

There will be regular frosts at night now, so make sure you add plenty of salt to the pond to prevent it from freezing over. Also, placing an old refrigerator, a couple of tyres or an oil drum into the pond is an effective deterrent against herons, as they are notoriously fastidious birds and will not approach a watering hole if it appears to be polluted.

Clean all garden tools and store them in a dry place until next year. At least now you can look forward to a few weeks of relief from carpal tunnel syndrome and tendonitis. Drain petrol and oil from the lawnmower before storing for the winter. Take care: this should be the last time you have to handle combustibles this year!

With Christmas approaching, it's time to plunder your garden for items that you can either drag into your house as decoration, or offer as thrifty gifts to your towny friends and relatives. The rule with country Christmas presents is: if it is edible, pickle it; if it isn't, paint it gold and stick it in a picture frame.

If you gave someone a pound of carrots for their birthday you'd be considered ungenerous, but at Christmas all the normal rules of consumption are abandoned. People will accept practically anything edible so long as it is colourful, chopped and presented in half a litre of cheap vinegar.

To pick the perfect Christmas tree, look for shiny green foliage. Shake the specimen hard for several minutes. Make a note of how many leaves have fallen off and repeat the process with the next tree. Don't be surprised if a little pyramid of pine needles gathers at your feet before you find the right one. If an over-zealous garden centre employee expects you to pay for all of them, politely explain that you only need one. If he or she gets angry, lift up your jumper, show them your 'Love began in a garden' T-shirt and walk out without making a purchase.

Plants received as Christmas gifts shouldn't be subjected to too much dry heat, and they should be kept out of drafts. Red poinsettias are, of course, the traditional Christmas flower. Put one on top of the television set and, with a little luck, it may still be alive by the time Kirk Douglas has been nailed to a cross. If your mother sends you a large bunch of mistletoe, hang it up high where the cat cannot nibble it. Congratulate yourself that your constant vigilance has kept your pet alive for another year.

As you perform your final garden chores on a crisp December day, stop for a moment and watch the many wild animals struggling. Everywhere animals and insects walk a tightrope of survival. You might see a robin or squirrel searching for food or a caterpillar in a chrysalis. Then kick the mud from your boots for the last time this year, come inside, settle down with a mug of cocoa and enjoy the playful antics of the cat nibbling pine needles as the heat of the log fire makes them curl and fall silently to the floor.

THOUGHTS FOR DECEMBER

Christmas trees are highly toxic to cats. Did we mention that before?